CEIVE

CEIVE

A NOVELLA-IN-VERSE BY

B.K. FISCHER

AMERICAN POETS CONTINUUM SERIES, NO. 188

BOA EDITIONS, LTD. 🞛 ROCHESTER, NY 🞛 2021

First Edition
21 22 23 24 7 6 5 4 3 2 1

For information about permission to reuse any material from this book, please contact
The Permissions Company at www.permissionscompany.com or e-mail permdude@
gmail.com.

Publications by BOA Editions, Ltd.—a not-for-profit corporation
under section 501 (c) (3) of the United States Internal Revenue
Code—are made possible with funds from a variety of sources,
including public funds from the Literature Program of the National
Endowment for the Arts; the New York State Council on the Arts, a
state agency; and the County of Monroe, NY. Private funding sources
include the Max and Marian Farash Charitable Foundation; the
Mary S. Mulligan Charitable Trust; the Rochester Area Community
Foundation; the Ames-Amzalak Memorial Trust in memory of Henry
Ames, Semon Amzalak, and Dan Amzalak; the LGBT Fund of Greater Rochester; and
contributions from many individuals nationwide. See Colophon on page 120 for special
individual acknowledgments.

Cover Art: "6 Step" by Elizabeth King Durand
Cover Design: Sandy Knight
Interior Design and Composition: Richard Foerster
BOA Logo: Mirko

BOA Editions books are available electronically through BookShare, an online distrib-
utor offering Large-Print, Braille, Multimedia Audio Book, and Dyslexic formats, as
well as through e-readers that feature text to speech capabilities.

Library of Congress Cataloging-in-Publication Data

Names: Fischer, B. K., author.
Title: Ceive : poems / by B.K. Fischer.
Description: First edition. | Rochester, NY : BOA Editions, Ltd., 2021. |
    Series: American poets continuum series ; no. 188 |
Identifiers: LCCN 2021009563 (print) | LCCN 2021009564 (ebook) | ISBN
    9781950774432 (paperback) | ISBN 9781950774449 (ebook)
Subjects: LCGFT: Poetry.
Classification: LCC PS3606.I764 C45 2021 (print) | LCC PS3606.I764
    (ebook) | DDC 813/.6—dc23
LC record available at https://lccn.loc.gov/2021009563
LC ebook record available at https://lccn.loc.gov/2021009564

BOA Editions, Ltd.
250 North Goodman Street, Suite 306
Rochester, NY 14607
www.boaeditions.org
A. Poulin, Jr., Founder (1938–1996)

for Ren

That a solitary person bears
witness to law in the ark to

an altar of snow and every
age or century for a day *is*

—Susan Howe, "That This"

There is a difference between after and after afraid.

—Gertrude Stein, "More Grammar for a Sentence"

CONTENTS

PERCEIVE

Val, you are a fool.
You hear a knock,

a thud, and sit up—
that's no neighbor,

no one is here, no one
is left—you are talking

to yourself, talking
to the inside of your

skull, talking to your
hands—listen, drift

back to sleep, back
to the dream there is

a vent in your chest,
six louvered blades

across your sternum.
A hand reaches in

but gets caught, cut
as it tries to pull back.

Gather your wits, girlie. You sit up on a pile of towels by the defunct sump pump—dead quiet, no hum. The basement is smeared with mud—in one corner, feces and mud—and someone is up there, in the kitchen. You hear a man's weight on the floorboards, footsteps that fade toward the north corner then stop. For a moment there is no sound and you watch the space inside the picture frame swell up to fill it. The frame leans against the foundation—that's the empty story, gray stones wedged in prickly cement, wet with groundwater, and you have been watching it. Then you hear the high pitch of a hinge and boots clomp down the stairs and he is there, a man, standing four feet away with his hands behind his back. Unarmed. Or his weapon concealed. He pushes a piece of candy toward you, which you eat. Who he is takes a long time to rise to the top of your mind: brown sleeves, canvas vest with pockets, shaking rain off his hat—Roy, the UPS man. *Get up*, he says, *there's a ship that's getting out.*

Recap

Frame: clicking off the radio,
dim Tuesday, dishes in the sink
from the night before—she had
offered to do them but you said

you both needed rest. You took
the sponge, said you'd try to call
her father later, California time.
Frame: you dragged the full can

back to the curb but hadn't seen
the garbage truck in weeks.
She went to school, wanted to,
and you watched her grab her

knit cap with the tassel, canter
to the corner and out of sight.
Turned back to your tea and list.
Frame: planes overhead, more

planes, dull booms from south,
sirens. Upriver—thunder, olive-
tinted sky, gusts, hail. Sparks
at the corner pole, power out.

N 41° 5' / W 73° 52'

You shake your head. You won't go. She could come back. He looks away, looks at the empty green bean can.

Recapture

Frame: shudder of the fridge fan
then out. Power out. You tried to
call her—no cell—tried to call your
ex from the landline—no dial tone—

pulled on boots and ran into the road,
your neighbor clutching a hoe, yelling
over the gusts about bombed bridges
and tunnels, bombs from planes, fire-

fight on the ridge. You ran—stoplight
out, swinging. You ran the metal steps
to the roof parking of the old diner and
onto Hudson Terrace, heard the rounds

from there, smelled propellant before
you saw. School gate. Kids running
along the far field, across the bus lot,
smoke puffs above the trees. Frame:

N 41° 5' / W 73° 52'

Roy looks around for anything useful. A length of rope. A hammer.
He picks up a box of drywall screws, puts it down. You tip forward
into a squat, palms on the cold slab. How many days. Running feet
went past the hopper window, gutters overflowed, water sluiced into
the well. You watched for sneakers that could be hers. Arms dragged
duffels. Your neighbor rapped on the door—*gotta leave.* Roar and
thrash, ripped section of roof, ripped branches, blown debris. No noise
for days now except the weather, thunder and gale. You're the only
voice in your head now. Days since the last truck, canvas flap drawn
back, man yelling *come on, come on.* No.

Recapitulate

Frame: screams receding, far afield.
At your feet, jackets. Jackets with kids
in them—face up or down. You reached
down the way you reached at her birth

before the birth was done, came up
with hands like that. Wind knocked
back: clouds churning over the river.
Frame: trumpet case. Funnel cloud.

Trumpet case kicked open, trumpet
a few feet away, vial of valve oil near
your foot. You picked it up. Sirens.
You ran back the way you came.

He turns to go and when he gets three steps up, you move. He looks back, frowns. *Two minutes*, he says, *I'll wait at the door.* You scold yourself: stop shaking. One tread at a time into the kitchen—shattered glass in the sink, wet leaves on the floor. You lift the faucet to hear the nothing, the choked suck. From the drawer you grab a pen and notepad, a Ziploc bag, a mini flashlight with a solar cell. Without looking, you pull her picture from the corkboard, flick away its tack, slip it into the bag, tuck the bag in your shirt. You put your hand in your pocket, feel the vial of valve oil there. *Left* means what's staying, and *left* means who went. You go to the door where Roy is waiting and remember what you said to her on her third day, when she was swaddled and strapped to your chest and you shaded her forehead with your palm: *this is outside.*

PRECONCEIVE

Val, don't forget about
type-one conditionality,
a habitual occurrence: *if*

*it rains heavily, the valley
floods.* Val, don't deny
type-two conditionality,

a likely occurrence: *if it
rains heavily, the valley
will flood.* Don't be sur-

prised if it turns out to be
type-three conditionality,
hypotheticals: *if*

*the whole world flooded,
I would build an ark.* Val,
you've known all along

*God regretted he made
human beings on the earth
and was deeply troubled.*

If you leave here now
you will never know
how high the water gets.

*As the waters increase
they will bear up the ark
and the waters prevail.*

N 41° 4' / W 73° 52'

Roy grabs you by the arm and hurries you through wind and rain with a torn Hefty bag over your head. Rain lashes your calves, your cheeks, finds a path down your neck—or sweat—salt or fresh. Along the river the wind pushes you forward, southward, toward the train bridge and the playground and the crumbled embankment. You turn to look up the rushing gully that was Valley Street—to the left, St. Teresa's steeple; to the right, goalposts. Smolder on the ridge. Roy won't let go of your arm, keeps your step against his step until you stumble into sync and your hips alternate with his, and you begin to move with a rhythm of footfall and splash. *Why did you make me travel forth without my cloak to let base clouds overtake me in my way.* You step over a park sign flat on the ground—Losee Field—white paint worn off the trough of the O. Roy pauses, takes a few whistling breaths. You mop your face, hear shouts—*hiding your bravery in their rotten smoke.*

INCIPIENT

A three-deck ship, neither
cypress nor gopher wood,

no portal or skylight—grid
of cell guides, sheltering

representative peoples
and animals. Overheard

instructions, received in
a dream or traffic jam,

injunction to build, cull
supplies, decide crew size,

hire stevedores to heave
crates and drums, traffic

in scraps and peculiars—
back to break-bulk cargo.

The righteous man waited
at a light as a tractor-trailer

slid back, but he was the one
moving, low gears catching

the future before he knew
how fast it caught the past.

At the end all things were
on demand, overnight and

bubble-wrapped by gross
and kilo: you were warned.

N 41° 3' / W 73° 53'

When you push the plastic back from your face, you see a gravel ramp into green water, then a bulkhead, then the massive red hull of a container ship. The dock is too small for it, and ladders have been improvised. Never seen the river this high. Roy nudges you to climb up ahead of him, past the words *CC Figaro,* each C as big as you. On the deck a young man is shoveling highway salt into a taller pile, his feet crunching around the edges. Two other men who look like him come around and cover the pile with a tarp, weighting it down with tires. A man and woman walk across the deck and greet you. Roy steps back, waves low, almost a gruff bow. *This is Nolan,* he says, *and Nadia. It's their ship.* Roy turns to climb back down the ladder, lifting one leg then the other, and leaves you there. They stand with parallel shoulders, look you over.

Receive

She'll need to ask you a few questions,
Nolan says. By *she*, he means his wife.

She says, *Do you need to wear glasses?*
You shake your head, look over the side

and see the pilings rise and fall. She says,
You look unlikely to conceive. You keep

your eyes on the pilings, shrug and say
you are 47. They look at each other and

Nolan says, *She would make the 54th*
adult on board. By *she*, he means you.

Nadia says, *We could put her on Crispin;*
she could shadow him. By *she,* she means

you. Nolan nods, then faces you firmly
and says, *Your job is to keep the kid away*

from the rail. You swallow but you don't
have anything to say. He says, *Someone*

will take you down to where you'll stay.
She's 334 meters long, 43 meters wide,

longer than the Eiffel Tower is tall.
By *she*, he means the ship, not Nadia.

Reception

That's the catch—
the dead weight of the net,
the last you'll see of shore.

You could jump,
survive the plunge from
this height and the shock

of cold water,
stroke back to rock, wait
for her wait for her wait—

one son holds
his ear to the receiver. *Not
getting any reception*, he tells

his father, rattling
the box. *No reception*, says
another son, a hair taller than

the first, reaching
to extend a twisted wire, *We
might not get a signal again.*

N 41° 3' / W 73° 53'

One of the sons of Nolan takes you down zigzagging flights of metal stairs. Your bunk is in Roy's container—bay 4, tier 2, row 17. Odds are starboard. The son counts off containers along the corridor. *Chill its chains.* The floor pitches, lifts and drops, but not enough to knock you down—you steady a hand on the wall. How much is on here, how much for how many: armaments, provisions, vice. You follow the son of Nolan with your eyes on the seam of his shirt, the piece that's called the yoke. From somewhere, soprano voices, then an alarm sounds above—three sharp honks—and he looks up abruptly, says that someone will show you around when they are at sea, plenty of time at sea. He undoes a padlock and holds a broad door until you put out your own hand, then he turns back down the corridor. *Where are we going?* you call out. *Farthest Greenland,* he calls back, *It's the new North Carolina.* What if there are already people there, you wonder— who is lost, who is left. You look in: this is your dark enclosure. Rises up in your throat, that dark does. With your foot you push a brick put there for the purpose to prop the door, lurch down the row past four more containers to the outer rail, retch. The ship slides into the dark mist, nudging past the abutments of the old Tappan Zee Bridge, straightening its course through the channel.

Capacity

Wind and watertight, holds
12 Euro pallets or 400 flat

screens or 200 mattresses
or 9,600 wine bottles or

48,000 bananas or 60 re-
frigerators or 2 compact

cars or 6 upright pianos or
1,170 cubic feet or 750 tires

or 69 bales of compressed
cotton, gin-standard density.

Economies of Scale

You'll get used to it, Val. Count containers
to find your way back, because nouns can be

mass or *count*, and some can be either—
sin, a sin, crime, a crime, death, a death.

Windward, leeward, athwart, abaft—nouns
occur in all environments, above or below

the waterline or Plimsoll mark, the depth
to which a ship can be safely loaded in a given

season or locale. Count the sons up to three—
turns out their names are Stu, Howie, and Jason—

count 67 souls on board: original crew, youth,
merchant marines, engineers, a few tunnel guys

from the Port Authority, fishers, builders,
craftspeople, pilgrims: Roy's their man who

had keys to warehouses—bullets, millet, rice,
protein powder, beef jerky, canola oil, nails.

Once you could call it a bareboat charter,
Post-Panamax with hydraulic rams and gantry

cranes, a quarter mile bow to stern, powered
by bunker fuel: what part of speech is *somehow*?

This ship's been through Suez, Guangzhou,
Singapore, Durban, Le Havre, Shanghai, flying

its flag of convenience for rent. In the heyday
of intermodal freight up to 10,000 containers

a year slid overboard in storms: a hundred gross
Tri-Metal Ancient Healing Power Bangles,

3000 Pac-Man ponchos on the sea floor.
The engine thrums through every pore, judders

the soles of your feet to the roots of your hair.
Step out for some air—containerization

divides the risk and limits the loss—auto-
motive to tilapia to zucchini, bay to bay,

tier to tier, starboard to port, let's say
I love you a bushel and a peck: proportionate

savings in shipping cost are gained by
an increased level of production. Go on—

the gangway has 88 steps, like a piano,
and they drove school buses into the hold

in the dark, fitted them with bunks. Firms
cannot realize economies of scale in perpetuity.

You do what you have to do. *Make rooms
in it and coat it with pitch inside and out.*

N 40° 59' / W 73° 54'

You watch yourself at the door: go on, go in. Shine your light and take a look around—two mattresses across wooden pallets, a metal cabinet raised on four-by-fours. You and Roy share a 20-foot standard. A bicycle chain coils on the floor near a shoe. You turn over a crate to make a bedside table, take the Ziploc with the notepad and pen out of your shirt and put it under the crate, then take it back out and slip the photograph between two blank sheets. You have half a little dollhouse now. You could make a table from an empty spool of thread, an icebox from a sardine tin, a sink from a thimble. The other roommate's gone, but he left his stuff behind: Jif, Ritz, DampRid, 24 wrapped rolls of toilet paper, an under-the-bed plastic bin, two paperbacks—*Private Eyes, True Detectives*—a tennis ball, a few perpetual candles—Sacred Heart, St. Cecilia. You know about night, and you can see it coming. You put away the little flashlight, its one spare bulb tucked inside, refuse to let your mind alight on corrosion or theft, then think the better of it and put the Ziploc in the plastic bin. In the corridor one of the sons calls out to brace for a stop. Commotion of chain on gunwales, hollering. *Then the Lord shut the door.*

Exceptional

They bring you the boy with his
muttering math and sextant,

hand you a leash and harness
in wind so strong the cord whips

your wrist, in wind that carries
the long crack of branches and

the rumble of lumber down
these bluffs where gusts twisted

four-story pines out by the roots.
In case you think you need it.

If he keeps lunging for the rail.
You cuff him by the upper arm,

but he's just shuffling his feet
mumbling *try the law of cosines,*

*adjacent over hypotenuse, even
not odd.* The rain picks up and

you say rain happens when vapor
is heavy enough to fall with gravity,

did you know that? You nudge him
until he looks: did you know *Rain*

is the B-side of *Paperback Writer?*
He nods and you think he'll be okay

but his eyes are fixed on the froth
churning out the stern. Turns out

everything with the breath of life
in its nostrils died, except a boy

with muttering math, son of the
plow, son of hazel, son of a gun.

The boy Crispin says nothing, stands scratching the eczema on his elbows as the sons mend a net, not bothering to ask him to step aside. *A few working instruments will get us out of the estuary without hitting shallows, then we'll need his estimates to stay on course in open sea.* They will take him from you at night, and they will keep him clean. The boy starts to fidget and you follow him down a row, where he finds the forklift pockets under each container, reaches his fingers into the slots as if searching for coins. The men at the bow give a shout and the ship slides between concrete masses, pillars of the giant bridge—now it's just the catenary, the swoop of its unloaded cables after the deck dropped. *Dire sea-surge.* The boy looks up and squints, then shouts: *find the area under the shaded region.* You pull him under the landing, try to get him to sit down. He swings his Nike satchel and dumps out his things, *commingled souvenirs and prophesies,* lines them up on the deck—a Florida magnet, a tiny Eiffel Tower, a blue spiky massage ball. You put the ledger in front of him, put the pencil in his hand. Go on, do it, do it and I'll play gin rummy with you.

RECEPTIVE

Yoohoo, you. Don't
pretend you don't know

who I mean—you are
the one who is still alive.

For now. Roy is also
alive, and you push

your mattress nearer.
You hate to want

a fishnet for a haul of
salmon, a fishnet with

a seam up the thigh,
your hand slid in to look

for runs, a rectangle
of cardstock to throw

away. He looks at you,
your eyes blue only by

comparison with gray sky.
He can't see your sweet-

tooth, your synesthesia
with numbers. You're

a good speller, passable
with a bow. He doesn't

think you'll last long,
but he lets you read his

skull for lumps, lets you
touch his cool limbs.

Nor can your shame
give physic to my grief.

Though you repent yet
I still have the loss.

The ship aims west-southwest to avoid the wrecks where the Holland Tunnel blew, steering around the rupture that sucks whirlpools over masses of concrete. *Salt-wavy tumult.* Everyone comes out and clusters at the rail, watching—girders, hoodoos, steel spires fallen to the canyon floor, concrete avalanches that came to rest where bedrock meets the sea, a new moraine. The city as terminal moraine. Crew stands every ten feet with guns, encircling the deck, some positioned on the bridge, but as the ship passes the southern tip of the island, they lower their arms. Two people lean at the stern, kissing and wailing. Crispin doesn't watch anything; he lopes and touches, runs his hand along every surface. Then he gets a sliver in his palm, fiberglass or wood, and it starts to redden and throb, so you take him to Nadia. She answers the knock and admits you to her well-lit and well-locked container—infirmary and dispensary. Creases between her eyebrows, cheekbones drum tight. When she answers the door, she has been writing something and still holds the pen, her long middle finger like the bone Gretel used to trick the witch. She has an autoclave, or just a stainless vat of boiling water, and she takes out a needle and a tweezer and, from a cabinet, a tube of salve. You hold him by the wrist, and the job is done.

RECEPTACLE

You speak a few dead
languages now, the one
of profit and loss, shock

and awe, vote and veto,
lingo of this place with
its cops and bond traders.

You still think in dead
languages, in the pursuit
of luck, deductions, but

the captain keeps quiet,
says too few words for you
to know if one or more

of his sons will want to
murder him. You guess
you'll wait and see. You

still speak it: shuffle-ball-
change, buffalo, buffalo,
spank—fuh-lap, fuh-lap

heel-ball-change, heel-
ball-change—bombershay!
Break, hop, Cincinnati!

N 40° 38' / W 74° 3'

The first time Crispin tries to throw himself overboard, you have allowed yourself to rest your face on your knees—you jerk upright, lunge and grab him by the thighs, take him down. He looks surprised but sits willingly. When he's been quiet for an hour, you pull Jason aside: was he this way before or after? *Both*, Jason says, holding his elbow at an L and coiling rope around it. *My aunt used to take care of him after school, the kid in the apartment downstairs who could do that mad math. Carried around an astrolabe and flash cards, OT every day.* You watch a triangle form between the rope and the two parts of Jason's arm. *She used to take him places on weekends, so he knew us when we came back, and he let us coax him into the truck.* You keep Crispin within an arm's length—the boy who could swallow the sea. *We went back after what happened on Martling when they raided the complex, found him bound, bit in his mouth.*

Analog

Kiddo, find Polaris while there's a break
in the clouds, determine the angle between
its position and the northern horizon. Or take

a measure from the pointer stars, Merak and
Dubhe, or the great square of Pegasus. Find
our latitude north of the equator: *in the event*

of equipment or electrical failure, get to port
by taking sun lines a few times a day, advancing
by dead reckoning to get a crude running fix.

If the star rises, we're facing east, if the star
sinks, we're facing west, or you can extend
your arms and stack hand over fist, each fist

ten degrees, or try the old kamal, one end
of the string in your teeth and the other held
away from your body, parallel to the ground,

even as the ground rises and falls, compass
and calipers sliding to the coaming with each
swell, stopped before they drop into the hatch.

A hazy sun will do if you don't know time
at local noon—a lemniscate, a shaded arc,
overexposure in the upper atmosphere, six

degrees warmer. You knew it would rise,
the sea, but not how fast, how fast you'd
have to reckon with the livid, visible sun.

Nadia walks with you to the end of a row and around another bend in the direction of voices. Someone strums a guitar. Howie and Jason are there, laughing, leaning on the R and O of TRITON. Two 40-foot containers have their doors open, facing each other. You look in and see girls sitting and leaning on bunks and floor—six bunks in each, like summer camp. Nadia sees you looking and says, *We are starting anew.* One girl screams *Marco!* and another kicks her shins. Smell of cocoa butter, candle wax. The sea roars in your skull. *Breast-lock.* You lower yourself to a crouch, hold your haunches. Your head drums *hold your horses hold your horses.* Crispin crouches next to you, tugs your shirt, worms a finger under your chin, so you drag yourself back to standing. The girls are tossing around a hacky sack, knotted red and green—under the crossfire of conversation you can hear the beans hit one hand then another. Howie laughs and Jason smiles sideways, strokes his jaw. Nadia looks at you hard: *they were alone out there.* You must have a movie playing in your eyes because Nadia starts to watch it, her eyes flickering like a train going past faster and faster, then she looks away. You look from face to face, from girl to girl, from head to head—none red. You say, *I thought the sons only got one wife each.* Nadia says, *That's just a story.*

Conceive

Take, get, catch—
catch the lining of

soft tissue, catch it
and grow. Gives us:

think it up, imagine.
Gives us: you get

what you get. Take
it again, receive—

seize, grab hold,
welcome, draw into

the fold, the hold.
Offer it up, recover

what was stolen. Re-
ceiver is what you

are now, recipient.
Here it comes again:

what if she wonders
why you didn't come?

When her hair caught
the brush you stood

over her, untangled it
strand by strand, held

one hand at the root
so it wouldn't hurt.

Concept

The god who can't sleep. The god who can't control
the population surge, who created humans but forgot
to limit their years. The noise and mess become over-

whelming. *With no comedy to speak of, God sees*
human behavior, regrets he made humans, overwhelms them
with a flood, changes his mind about how to manage

human behavior, and needs the rainbow as a reminder
not to fly off the divine handle at them in the future.
Miami in a blood moon, floodwater up to the chassis

of the Porsches. Not unheard of. You can't let investor
confidence start to slip away, can't keep up with king
tides—triple whammy, plus other whammies we have-

n't mentioned. The neighbors and reporters stood and
watched the sea as wind-driven rain pelted the sliding
glass door. The parking lot flooded but the mall is fine.

Not unheard of. Smart gods make special classes of
women who bear no children, let demons snatch some
babies from their mother's laps. You're in overdrive,

injecting resin into the holes in the limestone, low
pressure in the gulf. Not unheard of. No one is going
to want to buy it like this—river of grass, prairie of

water, interstate closures. If you make a fire to one god,
the other gods who smell it will become enraged. All
the world's knowledge fits in nine hazelnuts that fell

in a well, don't you know. The lucky ones ride it out
in a boat with sages, a fish revealed to be the hero,
don't you know, don't you know, don't you know.

Roy manages to corner the escaped snake and bag it in a pillowcase. There are fewer animals than you thought there'd be: pigeon, beetle, skink, goat, a ferret with terrible musk. Someone swears there's a caracal, but someone else says it's a house cat with a torn ear. Roy gathers up scattered millet with a dustpan, unjams a spigot, rehangs a door. A ship needs a cob, and a cob can be a man who can drive a truck, tamper with a carton, bench-press another man, or a cob could be a male swan, or a stubbly-legged horse. Roy's favorite currency is the old-style ten with Hamilton, and he whistles, and he has a habit of saying the second half of sayings: *in one basket, on the other side of the fence, I'll scratch yours.* After breakfast you go looking for him to ask how to pump the head properly, what to do with bottle caps, who decides who gets a length of clothesline by the fan. You see him coming out of Nadia's container rubbing his arm, but he looks grim so you don't approach. Nadia crosses her arms over her chest, watching him on the stairs until his head drops below the deck.

Except

You miss bathrooms but you don't miss
the Dyson Airblade. You miss ice.

You miss the oven mitt with its greasy char,
the cheese grater's fierce rosettes. No need

to reboot the router, run a finger through
fluff tongues of dryer lint, rip a jammed

sheet from the chute. Batten down this
floating planet with everything except

Next-Day Air, all-inclusive Yucatán,
pedicures, Post-its, zip codes, Visa—*visa*

has none of its meanings now—no cash,
no sprinkler head, citronella, dry socks,

vodka, nickels, heat, Pop-Tarts, shots for
measles, spam *cauchemar*: Ray-Ban chic

Cialis *Bottega Verde suplimente* Movistar
complementary hello: the odometer turning

thousands of miles, until the lease runs out—
you miss the feel when the steering wheel,

making a wide turn, slides back and clicks
to release the blinker as you press the gas.

Perception

The pepper specks are not out there
on the gray sea, they are on your eyes,

and so are the bodies, when you think
you see bodies out there on an altar

of snow, hatch-marked for contour,
their ashen faces delineated with

vented snouts like *Les Demoiselles
d'Avignon. Out of parsimony I took*

*whatever I found, because we were
now in an impoverished country.*

Take what you find—flagstaff, drift-
wood—take what you need from

what you hear—persimmon from
permission, footprint from input,

backhand from sandbag, or back-
fire, parachute, matador, hive—

you don't still see them, do you?
You thought you were alone.

Out there, on the sea surface,
smear is epistemology; affix is

ontology. You can't see it, because
it's raining, but you believe the moon

is up there, because there used to be
a moon up there that you knew.

That was Montauk. First valley, then ruins, then long days with a low smudge of shore off the port side, then it's gone—you're off the edge. The ship proceeds with caution, encounters a tugboat and exchanges a satchel for several heavy drums, the amber contents of which slosh on deck. The sons hasten to dilute the spill with seawater, and the ship begins to pick up speed. Nolan stands on the catwalk between the bridge and cranes, surveying the activity. You watch the man watching. You watch the man waiting to see what happens next. Commotion behind the forepeak tank: Nolan comes down, breaks up a fight. Fuel in the hull, fuel funneled to the engine room, fuel ignited in a steam arena. Piston-driven motion, tossed back with the westerly surge. Fuel: in your nose as fume, in your eyes as smoke, day and night, oil and fume and smoke. Each night pressing east, each night drifting from surfeit, from the memory of surfeit, closer to dearth.

Perceptive

Sea says alley-oop—sea is a poor
performance with a squeegee—

sea is a screen showing track-
and-field footage—sea collects

all kinds of clippings—toenail,
magazine, grass—sea keeps sanctity

in aluminum cans—sea is rain,
a whole lot of it—sea regresses

to gray again—sea is a piece
of linoleum with cuts where

a knife was dropped—sea says
persuasive, squander, sway—

sea is a nylon shower curtain
to catch drips and debris—sea

shows a fecal smear—sea is
mica, Masonite, wet cardboard

wadded up—sea survives
all its gunshot wounds—sea

is a quilt, dingy from a body's
oils, from dragging the hem—

sea is a hung jury, a psalter,
a heckler, a crone—sea swears

someone tracked the mud in—
sea stutters, tells it like it is.

DAIRY QUEEN

You dream of the tail of a fried shrimp and want
nothing more than to lick one cartilage socket

for a trace of batter and spice. You dream of
the smell of garlic on your fingers, the cloves

crushed under the blade of the cleaver under
the heel of your hand. You dream of unwrapping

a bodega Danish and licking the layer of crumbs
and glaze off cellophane. You lived at a time

you lived at a time you lived at a time when there
was too much to eat, when corn became candy,

when L-cysteine, derived from human hair and
duck feathers, was a dough conditioner in many

processed breads, when insect excretions found
in Thai forests formed the shellac that gave

jellybeans their sheen, when titanium dioxide
was used to whiten ranch dressing and protect

the skin from the radiation released through
a depleted ozone layer. Hazy now, hazy girl,

get out of bed, get yourself in line for gruel:
there's the man in charge, see him up there?

He climbs up the ladder to cross the bridge
and hollers down some instructions to one

of his crew, hollers his wishes, importunate
and incredulous, as the chosen always is.

N 41° 19' / W 69° 46'

You venture out, take some laps, don't make eye contact. Neither does Crispin; you get along well, double solitaire. He punches the calculator keys with his knuckle, converts decimals to degrees. Do they really need this kid who keeps getting the runs, far be it from you to question. Far be it. People have to stop looking at the sea, Nadia says. They're getting confused by their perceptions, the sameness and static, the Ganzfeld effect—here is there, up is down, foreground is background, blizzarded, minced inscriptions on the sea surface, rain-streaked sky. Stop looking out there, she tells them. Look into the palms of your hands for a while. Study the map. On the soup line, the guy in front of you says he's never heard of it—Nantucket—the land mass that used to be just over the water. Jason with the ladle remains unfazed. *Who needs Nantucket.* You imagine you see a shallow spot where the color is lighter, the faint breach of a sandbar.

SUSCEPTIBLE

You sicken, Val, or the sea sickens you, and who
knows what comes from the sea and what comes
from contagion—wait and see if there's a fever.

When you drift you dream of her childish fury
and your grip on her arm, on a lid refusing to
yield, a stalk snapped in half to fit in the trash.

Where does the duct lead? How far down it
could you crawl if you could pry up the strip
of screws and force open the grillwork?

The ship pitches on open sea and you hold
Roy's back while the rain beats the box, and he
whispers *mareada, mal di mare, mal de mer,*

brings you a capsule from a case he keeps
in a lockbox, but the word *dysentery* slides
into your mind, sparks panic—you have to

get out, gasp for fresh air, stagger to get
a look at the horizon over the olive sea.
Green at the green at the green at the gills.

Steady there, breathe, two hands on a piece
of PVC pipe. He follows you out, finds you
retching at the rail, reaches around you and

takes your arms from your sides and presses
his thumbs on the inner wrists, firmly.
You feel his neck bend toward your neck.

N 42° 54' / W 67° 56'

Roy at the winch, working his shift as the ship picks up steam, nosing toward the northern ocean, too far off shore now to see the mass called Maine, too shrouded in cloud. Roy reaches up to pull down a cable, revealing a strip of his belly. Conditions of rust, conditions of corrosion—chores and tasks at the tack, a fresh coat of red paint to mark the clearance for the hoistable ramp. Someone scrubs graffiti from a bulkhead door. Someone applies glue with a wide brush to affix a friction strip. Then commotion and the smell of smoke—a waft that lights hunger and joy and panic in you and in so many—there is a rush to the aft deck—someone has managed to light a small fire. The sons are on it and him in less than a minute, all three of them. Two sons pick the man up by the arms and one grips his thighs, and straight up and over they hold him over the churn from the rear engine, count to five, bring him back and set him down. *Not okay*, they say, then turn and go back down to the boilers.

Apperceive

The rain rains.
The rains rain.

The soot sifts
sootingly, grimes

the mind's sky,
muddies it, ashes

it dry. This is what
the dusky swifts

fly through, this
is where they go.

They won't go
back to a tropic or

back to a branch
where she hung

her damp cap or
she put her foot.

Rain on the roof.
Roof in the rain.

On roof the rain.
On rain roof the.

The on rain on the
roof. Roof rain.

N 44° 35' / W 63° 31'

Halifax, talk of taking on more diesel. Six cranes flank the port like giant giraffes, another leans to the left, tangled in cables, across a ramped roadbed. But the scouts say the harbor is abandoned—no fuel, no souls—only a scattered landfill and a gully full of mud. There's a broken hull, a ship run into the seawall and sunk, *Dole Chile,* its sunburst logo just above the waterline, stern marked *Nassau.* The expectation of activity brings everyone out. They crawl from the steppes of stacked containers, emerging from the high ones that require a climb down three or four side ladders to reach the deck, a wall of containers with checkerboard ends: red, teal, red, teal, red. Roy isn't around, and you find him in the dark in a fetal curl. He says it's all the years lifting boxes, the pain that corsets his ribs—*chafing sighs hew my heart round and hunger begot.* Then the alarm sounds and it's all hands, a shuffling of sheets, the rumble of engines, resuming course. When the work's done, you go back and sit with Roy awhile. He unlocks his little box, shakes a few tablets into one canister, one in another, one under his tongue.

Perceiver

Roy says, *Easy now Val, lie*
there and don't waste light.
You like his cool dry touch,

the lobes of his ears, the ash
in his beard, the way he finds
the mole on the back of your

neck and adores it with his
fingertips. You should hate
yourself for being alive, for

not being able to stop liking
being alive, for still loving
the dumb soup cans lined up

on shelves, the stick in a jar
that becomes decoration. Look
away from the flash recall

of a summer day he wheeled
a dolly up the driveway with
a carton of books, admired

her bike festooned with bows
for the Fourth of July. He says,
Don't cry, Val of Soul Making.

You listen for the pause before
his inhale, the little nothing, the
bottom of the breath that one day

won't come back up. Bless this
breath, Val of the crawlspace,
Val of the dictionary—you feel

his breath in fluid darkness, feel
it thicken, ease, swell—Val's
diction forbidding mourning,

or is it morning, you can't tell.
You never reach for each other
right away, only after you've

drifted off, maybe a half hour
after you slip into shallow
sleep, so touch takes place

on an island off wakefulness,
unattached to day, unreach-
able by foot or bridge, reach-

able only by an unmoored
vessel that tips and heaves
offshore in wakeful night.

Crispin sits and looks. You look and sit. You spy with your little eye a red balloon. You spy a rowboat with wings. You spy an afterimage of a scene: barbed wire across a cobalt field. Behind the field somewhere, the sun is giving it a go, and the glare begins to hurt so you look down at your body, still thick in the middle, even as the muscles recede and purple veins rise around your ankles. Your circuitry is starting to show. Nolan follows four men carrying sandbags, carrying one himself. He unties a rag from his belt loop and wipes his brow, a rag that was torn from a man's undershirt. The deck where you sit has a layer of gray grit on it, and you'd like to have that rag to wipe it with. You trace a finger in it, spell out *Val was here,* spell out *ant, antigen,* add to it: *antigenesis.* You look out to sea again, imagine a landmass until you think you see one. Somewhere out there a piano has been left to seed, because at some point, perhaps several points, the divine thought total genocide was a good idea. Maybe it is. One more virus would do it. Man and beast, man and soap, man and medicine, booze, music—man and the creeping thing and the fowls of the air. Save your friends.

PRECONCEPTION

The future in the past: he said
he would come back at midnight.

Come can never take a direct object.
Not: Roy will always come money.

Come can't be made passive.
Not: Early is always come by Roy.

While you wait, the mind's sky is
dirty snow, is the jagged lid after

the can opener has gone around
and pried it up. Are you between

saying and midnight? He said he
would come back at midnight, did.

You go with Roy and the sons to the container of a suicide to see what can be saved, to help carry. Crispin follows behind, tells you again the capital was Nuuk. Tells you the Danish krone found an ice-free fjord. Stu cuts through the lock, but it turns out there isn't much—Lysol and apple juice, a dog bed, no dog. Maybe the future has no dogs, no auks, skuas, puffins, buntings, sperm whales. You carry out a box with fuel canisters, the kind that would sit in a metal stand under a chafing dish. Set on top is a package that says CVS Elastic Stretch Net. A man in a mechanic's coverall comes up and interrupts with a report of a clogged fuel line and its subsequent repair. The group stands in the vestibule for a full minute while the wind sends up spray, then moves ahead single file with the boxes. The ship held steady in last night's squalls, the mechanic says, but there will be more, especially in the sea off Newfoundland. You shift your hold on the box, shrug your shoulder to rub an itch on your cheek. The most useful thing they found is a spade—Stu's got that.

Apperception

Deluge drawings: naked is
sand on sand. Naked clings

to driftwood. Naked looks
at the wall of your forehead

from the inside, calls out
for help for a short time.

Naked is porous, spiral force,
is pink fiberglass behind

plywood, is sheetrock, bed-
rock. Naked are days before

you identify the smell on
his skin as nutmeg. Naked

sifts through scraps, finds
tattered corduroy for a patch.

Naked knows how it used to
look. Naked knows that how

it used to look is what makes
it look like this, like blizzard,

like batter. Naked subsides
in tidepools, in calcified reefs.

Naked knows better than to
call it lace, that larva-eaten leaf.

N 49° 43' / W 53° 53'

Just off Joe Batt's Arm. Nadia's on the bridge, and you bring her the new calculations. *Narrow nightwatch nigh the ship's head while she tossed close to cliffs.* She gestures for you to sit, tells you things—drugs they can grow, remedies, interactions, techniques. There are more men than women of working age on board. While she talks, she oversees the change of watch, the steady steps along the catwalks and up to the crow's nests, the gray-clad backs bent over their tasks. The northern sea has begun to roll with more surge and menace, and a layer of chill under the mist clings to the mouth and nose, undercold. No icebergs to worry about anymore. She tells you that the continental currents are uncertain, as are the depths. Crispin has another bellyache. Some crew sweeps up a grainy spill on the deck below, and she stops to write a note. She looks up as if she has news and explains that the females of only two species undergo menopause. That is, the females of only two species outlive their capacity to reproduce: humans and killer whales. Experience in cessation: the females stop having young, then they lead the pod, carry knowledge of navigation, food supplies, routes.

NOCICEPTIVE

Three nights in a row you dream
you bite down on the pit of a date.
On the third day the pain is there

when you awaken. Nadia admits
you to the room, makes you wait,
like the old world, seated on a cot

under a shelf with jars of seeds:
arnica, aloe, comfrey, dong quai.
Rehydration salt packets, witch

hazel, Betadine. Boxes marked
veterinary supply, clamps and
forceps, cases of Israeli bandages.

You are afraid you'll have to lose
the tooth but she finds an abscess
low on the gum, lances it—salt

cream, relief—then exquisitely
sore to the touch of your angry
tongue. Relief tips significance

toward belief, blessing or hex,
her immaculate gauze, stockpile
of pills—sacrosanct in silica.

Something happened overnight and now the boy's afraid again, angry and mute, refusing to answer. You have to pry his fingers off the rail and drag him back. *Whatever shape it took in Crispin's mind, if not, when all is said, to drive away the shadows of his fellows from the skies.* He is greasy and delicate with downy limbs, getting some acne, and he gives off a sweet and rubbery odor like a deli case. Jason brings a coffee can full of pennies and an empty Poland Spring jug, and Crispin feeds the pennies one by one into the neck. When he is done, he lies supine and the language starts to come out of him again, the words *split up in clickering syllables, intricate in moody rucks.* You listen to him talk about the Cloaca Maxima, intestinal helminths and coliforms. The gusts pick up and he calls out about the Venetian *acqua alta*—sirocco wind across the lagoon! He sits up and draws a picture of the flood barrier, the control center in the chapel under the gaze of Saints Mark and Veronica. He shows you how the hollow barriers lie flat when they are full of sea water. Then, when the flood comes, they are pumped empty and filled with compressed air, so they rise up, floating into position to block the sea.

CATCH

Troughs catch rain
to drink, catch all

the rain they can
to bathe cook sip.

That's the catch—
wet in a world of

wet you wait for
a trickle to fill the

basin while a push
broom pushes rain

off the edge, off
a slippery surface,

while a raindrop
catches your eye,

then your throat,
while you watch

one drop catch
your lip, the lip

of the trough—
it beads up, then

flattens, smears
and slides into

your mouth, into
the tub. Mists,

thirsts: what are
your other thirsts?

N 51° 58' / W 49° 20'

You wake up before dawn and feel ease in your limbs, so you go out to look at the rolling dark. You squint until you think you see a cliff, a cave. You think about lashing reed to reed, then another to another, to make a roof. How tight it must have to be. As you move along the starboard rail, hand over hand, watching the never-curve of the horizon come into view in deep blue, you think about the geometry of a chair. When you reach the prow and start to move down the port side, you look up: on the stack ahead, Roy. His curved back, his calves as he climbs up the rungs on the balls of his feet. You stop. There is a wraith behind him: Crispin. When they reach the level top of the container, Roy urges him into the tight spot between stacked pallets; Crispin goes in and comes out with a package. Roy claps him on the back and guides him over the far side. *The natives of the rain are rainy men.*

CAPTION

A man throws a leg over a wall
and swings the other leg up to
meet it, drops soundlessly on
the other side, jimmies a lock.

A man descends a ladder into
the lowest tier of a freighter
and enters an engine room
with gold transmission shafts.

A man admires *a pure power-*
generating steel-made noise
and heat-producing cathedral.
In his palm—pills, raindrops.

MISCONCEPTION

Nolan is the hero of this story—he sets
its course. Nolan is a man with arms

outflung, a man known for being more
righteous than the rest, irreproachable,

a man who catches the windbreaker
before it's sucked into the whirlpool.

He's a rain gauge, a sarcophagus carved
with grackles and holly, a nude riding

a pair of scissors into Bal Tabarin,
a sapling submerged in limpid green

at Giverny. Nolan is a manmade tower
of twisted red and green wire, fiber-optic

circuits connecting his lungs and penis,
a man outraged that it has come to this.

Nolan is a girl dressed entirely in candy.
Nolan is the only man who keeps tabs

on the hatchlings, the only woman left
with her hat on. Nolan knows the devil

is in the details. He's calamity, crow. He
wants you to know he knows you know.

While everyone eats, Nolan and Nadia walk the rows from opposite points, their gazes catching each time they pass and reverse course. Each gust wears another layer off them. *Take by sevens the clean beasts. Take by twos the unclean beasts. Everything that moves along the ground. Everything with wings.* Each person's knees, cross-legged, touch another person's knees. Someone says, *where are the lions?* Someone thinks that's funny. Nolan says, not loud enough to be a speech but heard by those near him, *We don't need two of every species, we need two strands of DNA. There's a bioanthology in the hold.* Hybridize: yellow pea, green pea. The pot is passed down the row, the slotted spoon, then the ladle for the broth. Robust admixture. You try not to think in fractions, force yourself to derail an *if* clause before it gets up to speed. Nadia stands at the end, pad of paper against her chest—paper, while it lasts, narrow-ruled in blue.

Pitch It Within and Without with Pitch

Descend into the cells in the hull,
rags on the rungs because they get

slippery. The girl voices recede as
you go. You tried to keep rooms

dry, running your little white de-
humidifier on fossil fuel, tried

hard to dry out the wet earth. Now
you feel it on your skin, the life

of the next world, thriving on your
sweat, buzzing in your ear—let

it bite, let it carry your blood into
the air to inject another sleeper,

to nourish superior carapaces, im-
pervious to heat or fallout, unlike

the soft tissue you expose to day.
Never ignore a musty smell, lay

perforated pipe in a trench, swirl
the walls with Tampico bristles

dipped in sealant. There they are,
the egg clusters: gnat, worm, fish,

large fish, newt, bird, large bird.
Chance in a vial, Val, take your

time among cages, never stack
more than five high, never cross

the flood barrier, the blood-brain
barrier, stay in the shade, stay.

Aweigh just means clear of the sea floor, running her deep so she won't roll. Each morning the crew unspools the hoses—wastewater, bilge water, gray water, rain—to rinse away bird shit and yolk and worse. Nolan mutters *desludging*, thumbs a ledger and notes the days they drain each hold, numbered one to seven, in rotation. Your nose turns to the smell of pine and vinegar. You know there are stores of poison on board, chlorine. The hazy patch of squint where the sun is, behind the clouds, rises from your left arm, moves over your head, then descends on your right. For one day's arc, you note the color of the sky: cobalt gray, sallow gray, taupe gray, dirty-snow gray, glacier gray, disinfectant gray, dishwater gray, afterimage gray. In last light, there's one thing left to pick up and throw away—a urine-soaked paper towel. Gulls gulls gulls.

Catch As Catch Can

Crispin tugs on anybody to play but most don't
want him around their darts and targets, horseshoes

and pins. Roy teaches him Spit, and Sorry. Who
brings a game of Sorry to the end of the world?

A wise person. Who has a harmonica, who holds
the jack of hearts? If you want to know what's next,

find the woman in row nine with the tarot deck
(her name is Carly). Take your turn reading out

names from a phone book, a dictionary column
a day, pushups if you feel like it, ballasting your

body weight, collapsing in the sobbing alley until
they make you get up. Get up, get up, get a book

of mazes, dot-to-dots, get a piece of rag rope and
braid, braid some more, keeping the tension even

along the coil, counting whatever can be counted—
rivets, rods, disputes—tally them up with a golf

pencil on a tile. Time's up: it's your turn to wash,
scrape, paint, grease cable, scrub soot, save ink.

Make ink out of whatever bleeds, knit hats to sit
well down on the head. We go ten knots an hour.

SIEVE

How many minutes until the sun comes up?
How many degrees above zero is the water?
What if she's cold? *Suddenly I saw the cold.*

*Suddenly I saw the cold and rook-delighting
heaven.* What if she was *sent out naked on
the roads as the books say,* what if she was

riddled with light? Do you mean *enigma*? Do
you mean *as with bullets*? What falls through
those holes? What falls through your skull's

holes at night? Is it a riddle or a colander? Is
it time to get up? How long will you last?
How scratchy will the bed be? What will you

eat? Do you want a wet death or a dry one?
Are the dead this bored? How do you reach
the dead? How did you reach the dead?

The word *arrive* comes to you. And *turbine*. Nolan says that when you arrive, you will see who survived, who settled. You might have to move on to another harbor farther north, or into the inland sea. There will be no taking, no killing, Nolan says. When he finds a field of peace, he will say the word, and the containers will be moved to a hillside and welded with other materials. Windows will be cut. Closed-cell soy foam insulation, and, eventually, windmills. Some will be reservoirs. You will have to wait and see. *They are nearly indestructible*, he says, *resistant to mold, termites, fire.*

FORCEPS

Pick a card any card, pinch
it from the pile and hide it.

An alternative to passive
constructions involving *be*

are those involving *get*—
get drunk, get laid, get

caught, get kicked off—
though passive *get* can't

carry a state. You can get
creamed but you can't get

understood. You can yank
the snag, unravel the row,

pull a fiber from the skin,
but a tapestry is not a net.

An earwig's pincers, called
cerci or forceps, protrude

from its abdomen and serve
to intimidate and fend off

predators who would make a
meal of it. Jewelers, surgeons,

and obstetricians can extract
a gem from a bezel or a vein

from a tumor or a head from
a cunt. A hand with a tremor

chooses a single capsule
from a vial, leaves no print.

The sun is over the yardarm but the flasks are dry. Ferment: all the talk in the clammy commons is how it will be done—what fruit, what brew, what cask. Someone tries to make a skateboard hydroplane in standing water on the deck; Nolan makes him stop, says he can't have anyone going overboard when they might not be able to sight them in the swells, let alone get a buoy out. Nolan paces, surveys the grease and hairlines, the torn pockets and blistered hands, tries not to hear the gossip and disgust. The man who slashed a man in tier two, over a bet. The cook caught fucking the marine engineer, angering his erstwhile lover, who pinned her down. *A flood hero is someone who cannot reconcile himself to the world.* He asks if anyone has seen Roy; no one has. One of the girls repeats *Honda Honda Honda*, changing the emphasis, until another girl tells her to shut up, declares to Stu, *You have to get her out of there before she does something crazy.* Too quiet now. *Heard naught save the harsh sea.* Everyone watches the sky for auspices. Crispin settles on his heels with a pencil, his tongue out the side of his mouth in concentration, drawing a rebus you can't figure out: an eye, a bee, the word *is*, a hangman tree.

CONCEPTION

Now do you get it? By *get,* you mean
understand. You dream of scrubbing
sticker residue off a wine glass and

it shatters in your hand. You dream
of kicking apart an anthill, particle
and scurry. Then the dream ruptures

with buckshot and blood *the same day*
all the fountains of the great deep were
broken up, and the windows of heaven

were open. All flesh died that moved.
All flesh died that moved. All flesh
moved until it died, so draw a line

through the crosspiece, reckon where
you are. That will give you the point,
offspring, idea, the *ever-fixed mark*

that looks on tempests and is never
shaken. Where does Roy go during
the night? You struggle to your feet,

cast about for a seam in the side wall
to brace your hand against and hold
for balance, feel the engine vibration

from thighs to groin to womb, womb
with nothing in it, Val, not anymore, not
a thing left in there to increase or bleed.

N 60° 12' / W 51° 3'

Nolan reminds you of a guy from before who came to fix the car's cracked windshield—smooth face, soft voice, no smile—but he isn't the same guy, the one who fixed it in the driveway, told you to wait an hour before driving for the adhesive to dry, had you sign the clipboard, left. Nolan would do the same: *you can rely on it.* He never squints, keeps a pair of dice in his pocket but you've never seen him throw them down, revolves the two around themselves in his palm, clinking the cubes without involving the thumb. He gives out unripped rain ponchos. He surveys the damage. He relies on the principle of the thing, on regression toward the mean: if the first measurement is extreme, then the next will fall closer to middle ground—one outlier, maybe another that rolls away, but most are centered under the entrance point. *Must bide above brine.*

Accept

You know Roy is awake
by the way the air moves.
You can become familiar

with a stranger such that
strangeness is canceled
out. Or you can become

acclimated to the strange-
ness of the stranger. Catch
in his breath, he can't catch

his breath. You grope for
the valve oil and uncap it,
tip a drop into your palm

and smell—nothing foul,
underhint of mint. You rub
it on the base of his skull,

the knob of bone behind
his ear, over the taut cords
that roll under pressure of

your thumb. You pour a bit
for the other side. That's
enough. You tighten the cap

and wipe it carefully before
you put it back in the bag
lest it leave a little stain on

paper. The picture is there
and you extract it, aim your
light. There she is, you say.

Roy bends his forehead for-
ward and looks. He looks.
Then he draws back, coughs

hard, stands, reaching to steady
a hand on the ceiling. You shake
the blanket off your knees and

stand too but he shakes his head,
puts his hand out, stiff arm: *No,
let me go out awhile. You stay.*

In the morning the rain slows to a drizzle and the clouds thin, though the watchmen have their eyes on a coal-dark flank to the east. Nolan and Nadia come around and ask everyone to air out, a whiff of inspection under *bring out things you don't need.* Doors are propped; mops are pushed. The sons are busy re-staggering a wall of sandbags under the stair when Crispin darts down a row and out of sight. You whirl back and dash in pursuit, but he comes back from behind you, a complete 360, his satchel in one hand and one of Roy's drawstring sacks in the other. He yanks Nolan's arm, then stands behind the wall of sandbags like a counter, smooths it free of flecks. He takes out the little Eiffel Tower and turns it upside down, shows that under a black rubber tab there's a space—a space with white pills inside. Then he unknots the drawstring, pulls out a box: *Air-Tite Sterile Hypodermic Needle 100 count.* Nolan and Nadia look down, as if surveying his wares. Then he produces sandwich bags with pills and ampules—single-use vials, amber capsules, blue translucent gels. He takes a white pill carefully out of the tower—opens his palm and shows.

Deceive

A thief is a thief, and here
a thief is a traitor. Caught

and uncaught. Caught
catching, see? The hooks

get sharper and sharper:
crochet, shepherd, fish.

A pledge to one is a deed
to another and which one

is he? Roy had the keys
to the warehouses, keys

to the truck. They look at
each other, the captain and

his wife. They are surprised.
Roy had a soft touch—he

approached without fright,
rounded them up, round

the bend, round the clock,
round the world. Packets of

pills slide off the sandbag,
fall. Roy had a soft touch.

That's just how things go:
Uncatch means throw.

What's a ship without its cob. Nadia convenes Nolan and their sons on the bridge. You can see them through the glass, one jaw moving at a time, then more motion. The door opens and a shrill voice carries. Nadia tells Jason to take a lap. The rest of them stand waiting for him to come back. On the foredeck some of the girls have gathered under the ramp cover, and they stop talking when you approach. They've all cut their hair in bangs. One sits on her hands and hisses. Another has a goiter. Another girl has one hand over her left eye and keeps it there, even as she shifts her arm to let you pass. Roy found enough of them. Roy, man of boxes. Nadia bends her head to speak to Nolan below his ear and he nods without looking at her, looking out to sea. Who knows what else he did behind their backs. They had come to rely on him. He had their trust. Nadia looks at Nolan, says, *I know, I know, but he has to go.*

You find him before they do, leave
Crispin with the girls under the ramp.

Roy bends to the rail, so you crouch
next to him and stroke his arm, from

the fossa of the elbow to the hand,
back up along forearm to clavicle.

Eyes down, he coughs, flinches,
then murmurs—*I saw her, Val.*

You pull your hand back—you don't
want to know who he means, scan

the taffrail for another *her,* avoid
catching his gaze, but he takes your

face between his palms—*I saw her*
near the school, on the aqueduct.

So many were dead but she moved.
I thought she might be okay, sat

her up and zipped her jacket.
Val, let go of your hands—which

hand is clutching which? Which?
I carried her as far as Cobb Lane

but there was blood at the corner
of her mouth and I set her down.

Her breath wasn't right and she
couldn't talk. I got out the ones

I could. You lay your hands on
your thighs. The afterdeck tilts.

All the beads slide off the string, Val.
All your beads slide off your string.

INTERCEPT

He was coming down the street, he was
coming down the street to do the taking,
take the coming, come the taking, take

the ones he found alive—atta girl, watch
your step. Did you think any verb would
take an object if you tied it tight enough?

No honey, *arrive* never does, *arrive* is
always intransitive. You cannot *arrive*
something, only arrive somewhere. You

are thinking of *leave*, which can be either:
leave the house, or *leave the girl there,*
leave her. Got it down? Got it down cold?

You shake your head and shake your head. The ship has crossed the squall line and pitches in the swells. You lurch back to the container and scramble for the Ziploc bag, overturning the crate. You can't stay here. You grab a blanket, stumble back out into the rain and among the alleys and stacks until you find a flattened box with its flaps in a cross, a raft of cardboard, and you crouch under it on the aft landing behind a piece of old soffit. You are below the sight line, no sight of the sea, heaving with it. On the catwalk above you, the sons of Nolan move in a grim line, two body spaces between each. Stu carries a canvas tarp. When they are standing together in profile, you see them as her sons, the brow and nostrils, spines perpendicular to the ground. Perpendicular men. Pallbearer, seafarer, shroud.

IMPERCEPTIBLE

You hear Nolan shout
stand clear and stagger

to your feet—thighs and
hands numb—pull your-

self level by level up
rungs to the deck where

a crowd gathers. They
move out of your way.

Those tears are pearl
which your love sheds

and they are rich and
ransom all ill deeds.

Godspeed, Roy says
to those assembled.

He turns to you, lifts
his bound wrists then

they pick him up and
all you see is his bent

back. A leg thrashes
once, then nothing.

You look hard at
the dusky sea for one

more flash, but there
is none. An arm or a

wave, you can't tell.
That's all it took.

N 67° 18' / W 58° 25'

Benumbed. You are soaking wet now. You are shaking. You have to go
back in. You have to go back in there without his body and its *bitter
breast-cares*, back into the dark with his lumped cot, footlocker, flask.
The bicycle chain, each vertebra greased and grooved. He would slide
it between his hands like a snake. It's raining, harder now, with ice
pellets, slush collecting along the gunwales. You have to go back in.

But Shall Have His Sorrow for Sea-Fare

It's time, Val, push through—
that I on high streams the salt-wavy tumult

traverse alone—push open
the heavy door that holds your dark enclosure,

holds your sleep, push through
this turnstile between your mind and the sea,

the sea-tracks, since he pressed
a token in your clammy hand—you don't have

to wait for her anymore.
Now my heart burst from my breast-lock

after this after, *care-wretched*
on ice-cold sea these nights of storm-toss

stumbling not to an altar but
a window, a ticket booth with bulletproof

glass—no, not a ticket booth,
a ship's engine room, a window in the door,

a frame around the story:
pistons carry you forward, forgotten and

forgetting the forgotten,
this he little believes, who in winsome life

abides mid burghers some
heavy business, how I weary oft must bide above

brine, near nightshade, snow
from north—near nightshade, snow from north.

Your stomach wakes you, interior sun. What choice but to go out for chow. Nadia leans over, says, *Val, it was mercy.* You refuse to look at her. *We thought he was strong, but he wasn't strong.* In the corner someone has left a phone book swollen with sea foam, its yellow edge frilled like dirty plumage. She touches your arm and you shrug her off—old ball and socket—humming your television tune, la la la, luh LA LA. What's next, what's left, what's ahead of you now? *Disease or oldness or sword-hate.* She'll just have to *beat out the breath from doom-gripped body.* You tap your toes a little. She grabs your shirt. She says, *Stop it, stop it—listen. His tumors had spread. His tumor load was already heavy and he would have succumbed. Did you want to see that? He was not in his right mind.*

MISCONCEIVE

The meaning of *next* got into the cracks
between the boards—*next day next day*.
You dream the vent in your chest clogs

with lint, feathers, crumbs, like the nozzle
of a vacuum cleaner, dream Nadia looks
into Crispin's mouth and finds a gypsy

moth's nest. The next day you bleed. Wet
red on your fingertips. You have not bled
in months, have not yet bled at sea. A red

muscle contracts: leaks brumes, miasmas,
repertories. You dream you write labels
for gray leaf willows and common juniper.

Someone screams you awake just outside
your door but the commotion quiets—*there
are no big cats on here, dumbass*. Maybe

a goat got spooked—easy breeders, milk
makers, brought to ensure a new world
overrun by goats. You dream the future

perfect: you will have been bleeding, you
will have spent everything trying to procure
safety, you would have given whatever

it took. You'd have done it. English loves
to contract. Now there's a story to fill
the empty frame. Only one corner shows

stone, porous rock laid bare by subsiding
waters, last visible triangle of foundation.
Find the area under the shaded region.

Days little durable. Rally, relay, rely. You teach Crispin all the curses and slurs you know: stinker to shithead, twit to twat. He says *rat bastard.* Then he rattles them off, the changes: Australia's inland sea, Cairo swamped, Mekong Delta inundated, Thwaites Glacier broken free, Caspian connected to the Black, the Mississippi Bay extending to Pine Bluff, Arkansas. He speaks only in fact. When he stops talking, he looks at you like he's asking why the sky did what it did, so you say, *human pride bothered God and it kept getting worse.* He says, *Goddammit!* You say, *Exactly.* You want to turn around and ask him why he thinks the sky did what it did, but you are afraid he might know. Around you, everyone is preparing to build: sawhorse, miter box, T-square, axe. *Rancid rosin, burly smells of dampened lumber.* Soon. The smell of barbecue gives the deity a change of heart, and he promises never to smite every living thing again. Crispin says he forgot one of the changes: the spread of hardiness zones for crops.

Receipt

Proof of purchase:
a pronoun cannot

take an adjective—
no pretty blond she,

no scrupulous you,
no formidable they.

Deed of sale, note
of debt, debt comes

due, dew comes.
A goat roams into

your rote notice
of gray gloaming,

nudges your knee,
chews your sleeve.

There it goes again—
day turning to night.

The hapless it brays.
The rudimentary we

prays. Foolish you.
That goat got paint

on its face. That goat
got pain on its face.

N 73° 44' / W 65° 30'

You teach Crispin to spell *parallel, imbecile, vertebrae, porcelain.* He bows his head over the page, writes the words from right to left, down to up, coloring in all closed loops. When the wind shifts, the air blows cold from the north. You had forgotten it, but the word *November* swirls in your head: *hail-scur flew.* Crispin nudges you, ready for the next. You write down *prophesy, idiosyncrasy, zephyr.* He starts to lose interest, and you drag his knees again to the side so he doesn't trip the passersby—the girls, nubile and bedraggled, have been trotting to keep warm, taking laps in pairs and threes, quarreling, shouting insults and chants. One hangs back, panting softly. Her shirt is riding up—her belly rounding. Recollection of cold, as it comes into the nostrils, throws the talk on deck into anxious teeth-chatter, hectic cheer. *Hard ice-flakes.* Howie leads a process of moving seed sacks from one tier to another. They are ready to get on with it, to sow—unless the seeds got wet and sprouted, in which case they'll throw the moldy mess under the trees. Imagine trees.

MISPERCEIVE

Not there, there. You would think
you'd know where to look by now

to accuse the horizon of foul play,
to check to see if you're still alive.

Are you? Still alive and looking?
Looks that way, doesn't it. *What-*

ever shape it took in Crispin's mind,
it might as well be out there: the sea

is the sea is the sea is the sea until
it's toile with tortoises or a turnstile

or a roll of raffle tickets or a grid
of exposed rebar sprouting a new

foundation. The sea lines up tabs
like manila folders—right, center,

left. The sea leaves wide-mouthed
Mason jars hovering ten feet above

the surface—you could scoop them
with a long net, while he keeps on

looking, *when all is said, to drive
away the shadows from the skies.*

Nolan needs an extra set of hands and leads you down to the bird room. You stoop under the low lintel and step into the squawk and bleat, *the gannet's clamour*. He looks around and takes an exasperated swipe at a tray, pushing aside dried clusters of droppings, gray and white bits like lentils in marshmallow. He lifts one cage on top of another to get at the one underneath, puts in his whole arm, taking hold of a greasy body in the frenzied flapping, setting it on a stainless steel counter where its claws skitter and screech. You get a grip on a wing while he affixes the clip to the other. The bird puts its eye on you. Across the room, *the eagle screams with spray on his pinion*. The head twists and the beak draws a bead of blood and you yelp. Nolan sets down the clamp and rummages under the counter. That's what he does, this man: respond respond respond. *It's no accident: women take after birds and robbers just as robbers take after women and birds.* You put your hand in a big work glove. Both of your hands would fit into this glove, but then you'd be bound.

TRANSCEIVER

A loon flew over their heads
and was entreated to dive

to find land and bring it up, but
it found only bottomless sea.

Try again. Send out something
else, watch it flap out confused

over the stern and pause perched
on the windsock, then pump its

wings once, twice, rising higher
and banking into the updraft as

the haze starts to thin, shrinking
into a speck against altostratus.

*But the dove found no rest no
place for the sole of her foot.*

Now lie down, ear to the deck,
feel the engine labor. Whose

footsteps are those, whose tap
on your crown? Get up, Val,

look: the dove brought back
a rowan branch, traces of mud

on its feet. On its leg, a blade
of grass. The raven never returns.

Crispin shows you the place on the map—an inlet with two triangular islands at the mouth, then a strait between Qaanaaq and Narsaq, then an inner bay. There's a cluster of tiny islands at the far end, unless they are underwater now, and cliffs in a cul-de-sac. The *CC Figaro* will run aground. The dinghies will be let down. The gantry cranes will be reassembled and the containers, one by one, in conditions of tilt or slosh or crash, lowered onto the sand. The ship itself will settle, serve up its material piece by piece to structure windbreak or seawall. *The blade is layed low.* You go out to read the sea. Nothing is white anymore, not even the helm, gray splattered. You hinge your belly over the rail, watch the gray sea rise and fall, a mammoth animal, an endless tarmac, a patternless array of short frequencies. The sky brightens a bit—a wisp, a prism, almost sun. *It's not enough that through the cloud you break to dry the rain on my storm-beaten face.* You have no intention of going over and reach back slowly with your feet until your toes touch down. When you look over the side again, the glare has become uncomfortable. You don't squint up at the sky—there's a spectrum in a tendril of oil in the bilge.

CEIVE

Then the dove doesn't come back either.
There it is, in the distance, starboard:

low line of riverine green, the dim green
of a limp one-dollar bill. Everyone looks.

The green of locker, dumpster, succulent,
manhole. None of those—green of moss.

Keep watch, Val, watch that dim green line,
don't lose sight of it, don't you dare dream:

grass, salmon, kitchen table, a stone to scuff
a shoe on. You want to see an earthworm and

light a candle. In your head you hear the sizzle
of a converter and you say out loud, *Let it*

burn thought. He found you in what was left
of the house, Roy did. You walk to the end

of the cargo bay. There's a smear on the stair
where someone has stepped on a waterlogged

geranium, or a torn ketchup packet, or flesh.
You look out again, and it's still there, the line:

a smudge the shade of wrestling mats, pocked
barracks-green board, standard issue, river

under overcast. Everyone hesitates. Llamas
remember the rain and stay on high ground.

Fish outgrow their clay jars. The girls are
anxious to get out. As for you, Val, maybe

it's time to stand on your old cold *I*, but
what's the use of that feeble stick with its

knobs and handles when you've got *Y,* your
divining rod, which you will need. You ceive,

Val, you ceive it all. That smudge of shore. It
isn't raining. The boy tugs your arm. While this

earth remains, seedtime and harvest, cold and
heat, spring and fall, day and night won't cease.

Cept

Hey, Val, don't go back in there,
don't feel under the cot for lost

scraps of your scratchings *nor
eat the sweet nor feel the sorry:*

cove, covenant, coda intercepted
at the shoal, told in present tense.

Notes

The Old English poem *The Seafarer*, in Ezra Pound's translation, has been atomized and dispersed throughout this book. *Genesis* 5:32–10:1 also leaves behind textual shrapnel, though much of it has slipped through the sieve or been resorbed. Other source texts include Shakespeare's Sonnet 34 and Wallace Stevens's "The Comedian as the Letter C," and my thinking has been informed, pervasively but perhaps spectrally, by Timothy Morton's *Dark Ecology*.

"N 40° 51' / W 73° 57'" includes the phrase *commingled souvenirs and prophesies* from Longinus, "On the Sublime."

In "Concept," italicized lines are from Ingrid Lilly, "Five Flood Stories You Didn't Know About." This poem also draws some detail from Tim Folger, "Rising Seas," *National Geographic* (September 2013) and Elizabeth Kolbert, "The Siege of Miami," *The New Yorker* (December 21 & 28, 2015).

In "Perception," the lines *Out of parsimony I took whatever I found, because we were now in an impoverished country* quote Kurt Schwitters's writings from 1919.

A few lines in "Dairy Queen" incorporate facts and phrases from wall text for an exhibit about food at the American Visionary Art Museum, Baltimore, Maryland, April 2017.

"N 41° 19' / W 69° 46'" draws from Morton's discussion of the Ganzfeld effect in *Dark Ecology*, 79.

"N 44° 38' / W 56° 11'" has Joan Miró *The Birth of the World* (1925) in its peripheral vision.

"Preconception" and other poems in this book owe a debt to grammatical explanations and examples in Richard V. Teschner and Eston E. Evans, *Analyzing the Grammar of English* and Eugene R.

Moutoux, *Diagramming Step by Step*.

"Apperception" looks at Leonardo da Vinci's *Deluge Drawings*.

Facts about killer whales in "N 49° 43' / W 53° 53'" first came to my attention in Darcey Steinke's essay "What Menopause Taught Me," *New York* magazine (August 23, 2015).

"Sieve" incorporates lines from W. B. Yeats, "The Cold Heaven."

The first italicized sentence in "N 57° 28' / W 48° 1'" paraphrases Lilly, "Five Flood Stories You Didn't Know About."

"Conception" quotes Shakespeare's Sonnet 116.

Italicized lines at the beginning of "Accept" are from Morton, *Dark Ecology*, 92.

In "N 75° 56' / W 70° 50'" the lines *It's no accident: women take after birds and robbers just as robbers take after women and birds* are from Hélène Cixous, "The Laugh of the Medusa."

ACKNOWLEDGMENTS

I would like to thank the editors of the following journals where these poems first appeared (sometimes with different titles):

Los Angeles Review: "N 41° 3' / W 73° 53'," "N 41° 3' / W 73° 53'" (2), "N 40° 59' / W 73° 54'," "Forceps," "Receipt," "Transceiver," "N 77° 8' / W 71° 55'," "Ceive," "Cept";
Oversound: "Dairy Queen," "Receptacle," "Except";
Poetry Northwest: "Perceptive," "Apperception";
Scoundrel Time: "Perceive," "N 41° 5' / W 73° 52'," "Recap," "N 41° 5' / W 73° 52' (2)," "Recapture," "N 41° 5' / W 73° 52' (3)," "Recapitulate," "N 41° 5' / W 73° 52' (4)," "Preconceive," "N 41° 4' / W 73° 52'," "Incipient."

With thanks to the students of the Comma Sutra in Columbia University's School of the Arts for leading me to my favorite cranberry morpheme.

And with thanks to the editors who published pieces of this story: Keetje Kuipers, Liz Countryman, Sam Amadon, Daisy Fried, and Blas Falconer; and to Peter Conners.

This book would not exist without the heroic readers of its ragged drafts: Camille Guthrie, Carley Moore, Aby Kaupang, Julie Choffel, Simon Waxman, Bill Waddell, and Lisa Lynne Moore. The tale also benefited from conversations with Jenny Browne, Keri Bertino, Stefania Heim, Timothy Donnelly, Alan Gilbert, and Deborah Paredez—I am lucky to spend time in proximity to your minds. Love and thanks to Gina Vercesi for her advice about plot when I cornered her at her kitchen counter, and for her endless capacity for warm friendship.

Thanks beyond measure to John Allendorf, who listened to me hash out many things about this book while we were out walking in the woods, and who offered only the best response: "That sounds complicated."

About the Author

B.K. Fischer is the author of four previous collections of poetry—*Radioapocrypha* (2018), *My Lover's Discourse* (2018), *St. Rage's Vault* (2013), and *Mutiny Gallery* (2011)—and a critical study, *Museum Mediations: Reframing Ekphrasis in Contemporary American Poetry* (2006). Her poems and reviews have appeared in *The New York Times, The Paris Review, Kenyon Review, Poetry Northwest, Boston Review, Jacket2, FIELD, WSQ, Ninth Letter, Blackbird, Los Angeles Review of Books, Modern Language Studies*, and elsewhere. She holds a BA from the Johns Hopkins Writing Seminars, an MFA in poetry from Columbia University, and a PhD in English and American Literature from New York University. A former poetry editor of *Boston Review*, she teaches in the School of the Arts at Columbia University. She lives in Sleepy Hollow, New York, with her husband and three children, and is currently the poet laureate of Westchester County.

BOA Editions, Ltd., American Poets Continuum Series